Impartial Observer

A letter to a member of Parliament, on the conclusion of the war with Tippoo Sultaun

Impartial Observer

A letter to a member of Parliament, on the conclusion of the war with Tippoo Sultaun

ISBN/EAN: 9783337152390

Printed in Europe, USA, Canada, Australia, Japan

Cover: Foto ©ninafisch / pixelio.de

More available books at **www.hansebooks.com**

A

L E T T E R

TO A

Member of Parliament,

ON THE

CONCLUSION OF THE WAR

WITH

TIPPOO SULTAUN.

By AN IMPARTIAL OBSERVER.

Eſt modus in rebus ; ſunt certi denique fines,
Quos ultra citraque nequit conſiſtere rectum.   HOR.

LONDON:

PRINTED FOR T. CADELL IN THE STRAND.

M DCC XCII.

A

LETTER

TO A

Member of Parliament,

&c. &c.

———————

SIR,

ON the theatre of war, a reverſe of fortune ought to be regarded as a poſſible contingency, both by the conquerors, and by the vanquiſhed.

The former, magnanimous, in the moments of triumph, ought to be open to conceſſions from the vanquiſhed ; and the

B   latter,

latter, depreffed by calamity, ought to avail themfelves of alternatives, without exhaufting all the refources of arms.

On this principle the war \in India, which, in its progreffive ftages, refleded a luftre on the Britifh arms, may be vindicated, in its termination, by all the contending Powers : And the definitive treaty with Tippoo Sultaun, which exalts our national charader in the Eaftern World, may be pronounced, on our part, the refult of deliberate wifdom, and magnanimous policy.

The maxim, *delenda eft Carthago*, has indeed been adopted by fome fanguine politicians, who, having contended for the total *extirpation* of Tippoo Sultaun, are diffatisfied with the mere *reduction* of his power.

But

But that maxim, both in its origin in the days of antiquity, and in its modern application to the East, was neither dictated by honour, by justice, nor by found policy *. And the cataftrophe of Carthage, inftead of advancing the profperity, haftened the decline of the Roman name. Far different was the conduct of the Lacedæmonians in the plenitude of dominion. For when, by the fortune of arms, it was in their power to have annihilated the rival ftate, " Heaven forbid," faid the Lacedæmonians, " that we fhould put out one of " the eyes of Greece !"

This was the language of a difcerning people, capable of moderation in victory, and confcious of thofe political relations

---

* Vide Effays on the Hiftory of Mankind, Second Edition, page 286.

which

which give life and energy to national
enterprize.

A balance of power ought to be maintained in every fyftem; and the annihila-
tion of the Myfore Chief might have
proved deftructive of general profperity,
and inaufpicious to our Indian Empire. It
might have produced war between the con-
federated Powers, diffolved our alliances,
and involved us in a labyrinth of difficulty
in the divifion of territory, and in the com-
plicated arrangements of Oriental government, from which, by dextrous manage-
ment, we are moft happily delivered.

Tippoo reduced, is an event far more de-
firable, than *Tippoo extirpated*; and by a-
bridging his power, by circumfcribing his
dominions within well-defined limits, and
by cutting off, in fome degree, his com-
munication

munication with the Coaſt †, we have nothing to apprehend from his future machinations, or from his alliance with any European power.

The

---

† By recent intelligence, it appears that Tippoo retains *Mangalore*, and the extent of territory on the Malabar coaſt, that he formerly poſſeſſed. Lord Cornwallis, in an official Letter addreſſed to the Honourable the Court of Directors, and inſerted in the London Gazette, expreſſes himſelf in the following terms:

" The territory that the Company will acquire by
" the peace, will be conſiderable in point of revenue,
" though, from the wide difference in ſeveral ſtatements
" of Tippoo's revenues that have been produced, I
" cannot yet form a judgment of the amount; but, im-
" portant as an addition of revenue may be, I conſi-
" der it of infinitely more conſequence to the intereſts
" of the Company and the Nation, than almoſt any ſum
" whatever, that the overgrown power of Tippoo,
" from which we have at different times ſuffered ſo
" much, and which has ſo long threatened your poſ-
" ſeſſions on both coaſts with total deſtruction, has
" been reduced, by the event of this war, within bounds,
" which will deprive him of the power, and perhaps of

" the

The avowed or clandeftine fupport of France ftimulated the ambition of Tippoo Sultaun, exáfperated his animofity, and rendered him the declared enemy of the Britifh name. But that fupport ceafed with the revolution; and the new government of France difclaimed, in an early period, all connexions in the Eaft, hoftile to our

―――――――――

" the inclination, to difturb us for many years to
" come; whilft, at the fame time, I hope that our ac-
" quifitions by this peace, will give fo much additional
" ftrength and compactnefs to the frontiers of our pof-
" feffions, both in the Carnatic and on the coaft of
" Malabar, as to render it extremely difficult for any
" power above the Ghauts to invade them."

Until the arrival of the definitive treaty, we cannot ftate, with geographical precifion, the extent of territory annexed to the Britifh dominions. But it is certain that Tippoo, by that treaty, has furrendered to the Company, the *Baramhaul* and *Salem* diftricts; and to the allies, the forts of *Gooty* and *Balhary*; while the *Coorga* country is alfo relinquifhed.

Indian Empire. This viciffitude of things,
this unanticipated difappointment, morti-
fied Tippoo to the duft, and contributed to
give a more decided afcendancy to our
arms.

The fyftem of French politics is no
longer hoftile to nations *; and that circumftance concurs, with every other, in
ftrength-

---

* How different was the conduct of France in all
preceding times ! Lord Clive, in a mafterly fpeech delivered in parliament in his own vindication in the
year 1772, expatiated with ability and difcernment on
the views of France at that period in the Eaftern world.
" The noble Lord," faid he, " at the head of the Trea-
" fury, will do me the juftice to acknowledge, that I
" laid before him a paper drawn up fifteen months ago,
" in which I ftated almoft every thing that has fince
" happened, relating to the views of France upon the
" Eaft Indies. It was indeed impoffible for me to be
" deceived, knowing the preparations that had been
" made.

" If

ſtrengthening the ſtability of our dominions in the Eaſt, and preſerving them from all future annoyance.

Let Tippoo Sultaun, then, flouriſh in peace, ſince no longer formidable in war. Let him ſtill rank among the potentates of Aſia, ſince, by the reduction of his ter-

---

" If ever France ſhould lay hold of our poſſeſſions, " ſhe will ſoon add to them all the reſt of the Eaſt " Indies. The other European nations there will im- " mediately fall before her; not even the Dutch can " ſtand; the empire of the ſea will follow: Thus will " her acquiſitions in the Eaſt, if any can, give her uni- " verſal monarchy. I repeat, and I would have what I " ſay remembered, that the French have not given up " their deſigns upon India." *See the Debates of Par-liament in the Year* 1772, *publiſhed by* Debrett.

Suitable to this prediction were the uniform proceed-ings of France during a ſeries of intereſting events, down to the æra of the revolution, when the concert with *Tippoo* was inſtantly diſſolved, and all offenſive wars exploded in the councils of that nation.

ritorial

ritorial poffeffions, by the decreafe of his revenue, and the diffolution of foreign alliances, he muft contract the fphere of his ambition, and ceafe to be the illuftrious incendiary of the Eaftern World.

Preventive policy, which obviates future danger, is far preferable to that *vindictive* policy, which confifts in unneceffary retrofpect, or has no object but revenge.

Even an antipathy to Britons may be loft in the admiration of their glory; and the Sultaun himfelf, or the young * princes, (now under the protection of a conqueror whom they recognize as a father,) may become, in a future period, inftead of an ex-

---

* The definitive treaty figned and fealed by Tippoo, and delivered to Lord Cornwallis by one of the fons of the Sultaun, has already become the fubject of hiftorical painting; and different artifts are concerned in the defign.

afperated

afperated enemy, the determined ally of the Britifh government.

It is not my province to delineate military characters, or to enter minutely into the detail of arms. To do juftice to the tranfactions of the campaign, would require the recording pen of an hiftorian converfant in modern tactics, and not unacquainted with the eloquence of antiquity *.

That affociation of talents which, it is allowed, belong to Tippoo, forms, perhaps, the beft criterion, by which we may judge of the merit of his conqueror. For *Tippoo* is not only fuperior in enterprize to all the monarchs of the Eaft, but many

---

* Res geftæ regumque ducumque, & triftia bella,
Quo fcribi poffent numero monftravit Homerus.

HOR.

features

features of his character might be exhibited
in the picture of an Achilles.

Impiger, iracundus, inexorabilis, acer ;
Jura neget fibi nata, nihil non arroget armis.

Lord Cornwallis then, with the olive
branch in one hand, and with the fword in
the other, has appeared in the fcene, during the whole period of hoftilities, in all
the fplendor of greatnefs.

To control the genius of defpots, is the
nobleft effort of heroifm. It is *the confum-
mation devoutly to be wifhed.*——It is *the
pride, the pomp, and circumftance of glorious
war.*

But it is contended by fome politicians,
that the capture of *Seringapatam* was fo
eafily practicable by our victorious arms,
that it ought to have been accomplifhed, as

the

the decifive blow, which would have entitled us to conceffions of ftill greater magnitude from Tippoo Sultaun, without the
total demolition of his power.

To this it may be anfwered, That certain
pecuniary ftipulations in the treaty, may
be rightly confidered as a *ranfom* for the
Myfore capital... And furely, a higher ranfom was to be expected for its prefervation,
than could have been demanded for its
reftitution under defolation and ruin. Yet
had we ftormed the Myfore capital, with
full affurance of fuccefs, our army muft
foon have abandoned it fpontaneoufly,
without ranfom or redemption.

The peace then, and the war, in every
point of view, happily correfpond. In policy and in arms we ftand in equal eftimation; and the Governor General of India,

in

in his civil and in his military capacity, deferves accumulated praife.

But it has been alleged by the difcontented, that the peace under review, originated entirely from the India Board; and, confequently, that the inftructions from home muft relieve Lord Cornwallis from his refponfibility, as they have tended to eclipfe his glory.

How far the inftructions from home directed the proceedings, or dictated the ultimate policy of the Governor General, we prefume not to decide; but between his Lordfhip and the India Minifter there feem to have exifted a coincidence and harmony of opinion, which, without running invidious parallels, may be pronounced, in their refpective departments, equally honourable for both.

A rupture

A rupture in Europe, in which **Great
Britain** had been involved, muſt have
greatly augmented the embarraſſments of
an Indian war. Whatever apprehenſions,
therefore, were entertained of ſuch a rupture during the late armaments, were, no
doubt, announced to Lord Cornwallis by
the India Miniſter; nor would he ſuppreſs
from his Lordſhip ſuch inſtructions on
that ground, as were dictated by the wiſdom of his Majeſty's counſels.

The ſtanding order from home, it
is probable, allowed the Noble Warrior in
the Eaſt conſiderable latitude. The Miniſter might have aſſumed an exalted tone,
and emulated Roman greatneſs:

> Hæ tibi erunt artes, pacifque imponere morem,
> Parcere ſubjectis, & debellare ſuperbos.

But the particular dictates of the Cabinet
on that occaſion, it were unneceſſary to
explore. The merit of the India Miniſter
reſts

refts not on any fingle event, or on any precarious ground ; for the whole fyftem of his India arrangements, from the efta-blifhment of the Board of Control to the prefent day, has been conducted with un-rivalled abilities, profound difcernment, and comprehenfive policy. During that period, our India fettlements have flourifhed in their interior government, in commerce, and in revenue, with progreffive and un-exampled profperity.

The reafoning of Mr. Dundas in his India budgets, which has been fo loudly controverted, feems now to be ftrengthened and confolidated in the public mind. The accomplifhment of his predictions on the fcore of finance, will, it is probable, be ac-celerated beyond expectation ; and our Na-tional Debt, inftead of being loaded with additional incumbrance, is likely to derive

feafonable

feafonable relief from our dominions in the Eaft.

The fcene which is now opened by the definitive treaty, could hardly have been anticipated by human difcernment; and by the extenfion of territory, the increafe of revenue, and the ftability of our poffeffions, we may venture to affirm, that India Stock, notwithftanding its temporary depreffion, muft, on every principle of calculation, rife to an unprecedented ftandard.

All Government funds muft be more or lefs affected by the fame caufe, and experience, in different proportions, a correfponding elevation.

This infeparable connexion of things muft be regarded with univerfal fatisfaction by every clafs of citizens; for the flourifhing

ing condition of the Public Funds will admit of the gradual reduction of thofe taxes that are moft burthenfome to the great body of the people.

This is a fair prefage of general felicity; and Great Britain, by its acquifition of dominion, of revenue, and of power, muft rife in the fcale of nations.

But it is not on Oriental ground alone, that we contemplate growing profperity.

Without entering into the details of financial ftatement, or comparing the public income and expenditure, agreeably to the report of the Select Committees, it may be maintained with confidence, that the Public Revenue of this country, by the induftry of the people and the increafe of commerce, is in a condition eminently flourifhing.

D   Whether

Whether the plan purfued by Mr. Pitt from the year 1786, is the moft powerful and efficient which could have been devifed or adopted in financial œconomy, is a queftion which we have not leifure, though we had ability, to difcufs; but the eftablifhment of that plan, it is allowed, has been productive of confiderable advantage *. Commerce,

it

---

* Even Mr. Morgan, who condemns, on mathematical ground, the plan of finance adopted by Mr. Pitt, from its comparative inefficiency, makes fome conceffion, and denies not the exiftence of fome pofitive advantage. "Admitting," fays he, "that by the reduc-
"tion of the *four per cents*, or by a *real* furplus in the
"revenue, the fum of 200,000 l. may be fairly added
"to the million already appropriated for the difcharge
"of the National Debt, I fee no great matter for
"triumph in fuch an addition. Its operations are al-
"together inconfiderable, and the whole plan is ftill
"weak and ineffectual. Compared, however, with
"what Mr. Pitt at firft intended to have eftablifhed, it
"deferves refpect; and though enfeebled and mutilated
"by his alterations, *it has done fo much good*, that we
"have

it is alfo allowed, has had a gradual increafe; yet this, it is contended, is not
peculiar to Britain, and is fhared only in
common with other nations.

On the balance of trade we mean not to
expatiate. But public credit in this country might be ftill farther illuftrated from
the relative condition of other ftates.

The neutrality which, in the prefent con-
vulfion on the continent of Europe, has
been avowed by the court of Britain, is ma-
nifeftly calculated to give us, ultimately,
additional weight and preponderation in
the general fyftem. While other European
nations are exhaufting their revenue and

" have only to regret, that the other more powerful
" and efficient plan, which had been fo ftrongly re-
" commended by Dr. Price, was not adopted."——
See *A Review of Dr. Price's Writings, on the
Subject of the Finances of this Kingdom, by W. Morgan,* F. R. S.

their

their blood, under a precarious deftiny; while their governments may be fhaken to their foundations, may enlarge or contract their limits by the fortune of arms, may be torn afunder by inteftine commotions, or be overwhelmed by foreign irruptions; the Sovereign of this free country may be looked up to by the belligerent powers, as the reftorer of tranquillity, as the arbiter of contending nations; while the venerable fabric of our Conftitution, fecure from danger, will excite the envy of the world.

Britons, however, are too magnanimous to erect their triumphal arch on the bafis of general calamity; they fcorn to aim at greatnefs by the depreffion of other ftates, or even to indulge the fentiment of Epicurean philofophy :

Suave mari magno————
Suave etiam belli certamina magna tueri,
Per campos inftructa, ulla fine parte pericli. Lucret.

The

The Revolution in France, counteracted by a confederacy of potentates, and so alarming to the jealousy of the continental princes, forms an æra in civil history, intimately connected with the future destiny of the world.

But in this country, similar jealousies are not likely to arise. Between the *noblesse* of France, and the nobility of Great Britain, there is so little analogy, that nothing in the French Revolution can create any well-founded alarm. Our nobles are regarded with complacency by the other orders, and are often distinguished in the Hereditary Senate, as the guardians and patrons of freedom. The Peers of the Realm then, and the Princes of the Blood, in all their privileges and immunities stand equally secure. But it is not France alone which we have to contemplate seriously, at this moment, in the drama of Europe.

The

The fame concert of continental Princes, the fame confederacy of the Northern Powers, which was formed originally againft France, is now formed againft Poland*, and feems to involve in it a plan of univerfal

---

* In Poland, the Nobility, by the dereliction of ufurped pre-eminence, have ingratiated themfelves with the People ; all is harmony within, and the new conftitution feems to be erected on folid foundations. It is even profeffedly modelled on the conftitution of this country, and on that account feems to claim, by a right of filiation, the fympathy and the aid of Britons. Mr. Burke has difcriminated between the Revolution in France and that in Poland ; and while he execrates the one Revolution, he allows the other all manner of applaufe. " In contemplating," fays he, " that change, humanity " has every thing to rejoice and to glory in, nothing to " be afhamed of—nothing to fuffer. Not one man in- " curred lofs, or fuffered degradation ; all, from the " king to the day-labourer, were improved in their " condition ; every thing was kept in its place and " order ; but in that place and order, every thing was " bettered."

The fubfcription opened in this country in fupport of Poland, is decifive of the fenfe of a generous Public,

who

universal defpotifm, which cannot be regarded with indifference in a land of freedom.

The court of Britain, in a public declaration to France *, has, with equal policy and justice, difavowed all interference with her interior government; and fuch interference (which is incompatible with the rights of nations) muft ever, we truft, be execrated in the councils of a Patriot King, whofe prerogatives are not only recognifed, but revered by his people.

Anarchy is not to be confounded with liberty, no more than defpotifm is with government; and, in our general policy, we ought to fteer a middle courfe between *Scylla* and *Charybdis*.

---

who commiferate the calamities of an injured people, contending for the unalienable rights of mankind. No power on earth will be permitted to triumph over

" *Th' unconquerable mind, and freedom's holy flame.*"

* See a State Paper by Lord Grenville.

" Liberty

" Liberty is a plant," faid a late illuftrious Statefman *, who long fuftained the
vigour of our Public Councils, and adorned
our Senate, " Liberty is a plant that de-
" ferves to be cherifhed. I love the tree,
" and wifh well to every branch of it.
" Like the vine in the Scripture, it has
" fpread from eaft to weft, has embraced
" whole nations with its branches, and
" fheltered them under its leaves."

The Son of that Great Man, the prefent
Minifter, whofe exalted genius is un-
eclipfed even by his father's name, has run
the race of popularity in the upper departments of government, and maintained it
even in the zenith of his power †.

The

---

* Vide a Speech by the Earl of Chatham in the year
1770.

† The following paffage, in *Effays on the Hiftory of*
Mankind, firft appeared in the year 1781 :—" We
have

The Leader of Oppofition, the Ex-Mi-
nifter, it muft likewife be admitted, is dif-
tinguifhed by pre-eminence of talents, and
ranks high in the eftimation of his country
and of mankind.

" have feen a Patron of Freedom in our days, inferior
" to no Roman name, commanding the applaufe of
" Senates, fuftaining the vigour of Public Councils,
" and leading on a nation to glory. We have feen
" another, of congenial fpirit, prefiding in the Affem-
" bly of the Nobles, and difpenfing, from the higheft
" Tribunal, juftice to the people ;
" ————His dantem jura Catonem.
" I dare not mention a name among the living—but
" that the moft illuftrious Statefman of the prefent
" age has left pofterity, is matter of general fatisfac-
" tion to the Englifh nation.

" The genius of that Great Man, furviving in his
" Race, and cherifhed by the fond predilection of a ge-
" nerous Public, may ftill be ufeful to his country ;
" and if we may judge from fome late appearances,
" the prayer of his contemporaries is already heard by
" indulgent Heaven ;

" *Stet fortuna domus, & avi numerentur avorum.*"

E   On

On a queſtion, therefore, of the firſt magnitude in politics, that affects the general ſyſtem of the world, a coincidence of opinion may be expected between ſuch luminous Politicians; and ſhould Great Britain be called upon, by future contingencies in the continental ſcene, to interpoſe in arms, ſhe will interpoſe, in all probability, with the decided approbation of thoſe Stateſmen, ſanctioned by the union of parties, and by the voice of the people. But if we may judge from appearances, ſhe is likely to interpoſe rather by counſel, than by arms.

The cloud which hangs tremendous over Europe may, perhaps, be diſſipated without any general exploſion; and at preſent it ſeems only incumbent on Miniſters, without deviating from neutrality, to exerciſe vigilance and circumſpection. But if, contrary

trary

trary to appearances, it is found expedient for us to open the TEMPLE OF JANUS, which has hitherto been kept ſhut by ſound policy, it will be opened, with unanimous conſent, by the hand of juſtice and of wiſdom, not in ſupport of anarchy, but of the liberties of mankind.

" On ſome occaſions," ſaid the great Monteſquieu, " it may be neceſſary to draw " a veil, *for a while*, over liberty, as it was " cuſtomary to veil the ſtatues of the gods." But that veil muſt ſoon be removed by the progreſs of civilization, and the diffuſion of arts and ſciences; nor will it be conſidered by Britons as a ſupererogatory duty, to ſupport the cauſe of the preſent, and of future generations.

Such is my mode of thinking on the ſubject of our National Proſperity, which I have

contemplated

contemplated with pleafure, in the definitive treaty with the Sultaun—in the mea-
fures of government—and in the com-
plexion of the times.

Such is the refult of general reafoning,
which, unfuggefted by Minifters, or by
Oppofition, or by any Party in the State,
has originated in fair fpeculation; and,
under the impulfes of patriotifm and phi-
lanthropy, is now addreffed to you, Sir, as
a Member of the Senate, and delivered to
the Public, by

AN IMPARTIAL OBSERVER.

APPENDIX.

THE materials for difcufling India politics are not always exhaufted in the
official information communicated to the
public. Other information from the Eaft
may be equally authentic. And as the
narrative of facts derived from unofficial
correfpondence is often enriched with folid
obfervation and judicious comments, the
following felection is here fubjoined, in the
form of an Appendix.

N°

N° I.

" *Madras*, 15*th March*, 1792.

" In the view of enlarged policy, it is
" advantageous to the fecurity of India,
" that a power refpectable, but not dan-
" gerous, fhould exift in the Myfore
" country.

" Tippoo, with half the territory he
" poffeffed before, will keep the *Marattas*
" and the *Nizam* in awe, at the fame time
" that he will ftand much in fear of our
" all-powerful ftrength, which has hum-
" bled him to the very duft.——With
" regard to advantages territorial and pe-
" cuniary, we could not have expected
" more, had we taken the Fort. In mo-
" ney, we fhould, probably, in that view,
" have

" have fallen confiderably fhort; for this
" is an article which might have been
" eafily carried away, in defiance of all our
" efforts. Every circumftance, therefore,
" unites to throw an uncommon brilliancy
" round the whole tranfaction."

***

Nº II.

" *Madras, 24th Feb.* 1792.

" I am glad to find by Mr. Dundas's
" laft India budget, that he has formed fo
" juft an opinion of the extra-expence of
" the war, which has been exaggerated by
" others beyond all bounds. I think it
" has not exceeded two crore and fixty
" lacks of rupees of extra-expence; and as
" the arrears are very inconfiderable, and
" the war muft very foon be terminated,

" the

" the whole will probably not exceed three
" millions fterling. Large as this fum
" is, it is not in proportion to the force
" we have in the field, or half the expence
" of former wars, particularly the laft."

As this intelligence from Madras is derived from refpectable authority, and cor-
refponds with Mr. Dundas's ftatement in
the budget of the former year, it may be
conducive to the farther illuftration of this
important fubject, to compare, with the
above India letter, the following paffages
from the fpeech delivered by Mr. Dundas,
on the finances of the Eaft-India Company,
before the Committee of Parliament, on
the 5th of June 1792,

" Inftead of the Company's finances be-
" ing oppreffed by the heavy burthen of
" five, fix, or twelve millions, which fome
" Gentle-

" Gentlemen fo pathetically lamented laft
" year, the firft year's war leaves thofe fi-
" nances nearly in the fame ftate at its clofe,
" as at its commencement; and if a confider-
" able allowance be made for any deficiency
" in the ftatements from India, it appears
" that not more than half a million ought
" to be charged againft the general ftate of
" the Company's affairs.

" It will, undoubtedly, be expected that
" fome eftimate fhould be given of the
" expence that may probably be incurred
" by this time in the profecution of the
" war, or, more properly, as the accounts
" are made up annually, what effect it
" would have had on the Company's
" finances on the 30th of April laft. But
" a general eftimate of this kind, can-
" not be made from the accounts received
" from India.

F   " But,

" But, without having recourfe to com-
" putations, it may be fairly fuppofed,
" that the refult of the fecond year of the
" war, will not be worfe than the firft.
" For, in the firft place, it is to be ob-
" ferved, that a large quantity of ftores
" and provifions had been provided in
" 1790-91, which were not expended in
" that year, but were applicable to fupply
" the army in the following year 1791-2.

" General Abercromby particularly ftates
" that he had rice fufficient for 40,000
" men for five months, exclufive of what
" would be neceffary for his army during
" the monfoon. This muft have occafioned
" a large expenditure in that year, which,
" it is probable, would caufe a proportional
" faving in the enfuing year. And with
" refpect to the other articles of expence,
" there is no reafon for fuppofing that they

" will

" will have been greater in 1791-2, than
" they were in the preceding year.

" Upon the whole, upwards of a mil-
" lion will become applicable to the ex-
" pences of the war, pofterior to the clofe
" of the actual accounts, which have
" formed the principal part of the prefent
" difcuffion.

" To this I am entitled to add another
" refource, or rather a diminution of ex-
" pence, which will afford aid to the fame
" purpofe, and which did not occur in the
" former year. I mean, a fum of be-
" tween two and three hundred thoufand
" pounds annually fent from Bengal to
" China; but which, by the difpatches
" that have gone out this feafon, is di-
" rected not to be fent thither in the enfu-
" ing year; the fullnefs of the Treafury

" at

" at Canton, and the increase of exports
" from this country, having rendered this
" resource for the China investment at pre-
" sent unnecessary.

" Considering all the circumstances which
" I have explained to the Committee, re-
" lative to the state of the Company's
" finances in India at the close of the
" year 1790-91, I feel myself warranted
" in believing, that the expences of the
" year 1791-2 will not exceed those of
" the preceding year; and if this belief be
" well founded, it follows, that the interest
" of the burthen on the revenues of India
" during this year, will be considerably less
" than was made in 1790-91; because so
" large a portion of the expences has been
" provided for by the resources above al-
" luded to.

" I shall

" I ſhall not detain the Committee
" longer; but to ſave any Gentleman the
" trouble of putting the queſtion to me,
" Whether I adhere to the hopes I gave
" laſt year, ' that the day is much nearer
" when the reſources of India will ad-
" miniſter aid to the revenues of this coun-
" try, than that on which we are to appre-
" hend that India will call for aid from
" the finances of Great-Britain ?' I anti-
" cipate the queſtion, and anſwer in the
" affirmative; and the only difference is,
" that I am more ſanguine in thoſe hopes
" than I was at the time I firſt expreſſed
" them."

Our finances in India muſt now flouriſh,
far beyond even the anticipations of Mr.
Dundas, ſince it appears from the laſt offi-
cial information tranſmitted to the Court of
Directors by Sir Charles Oakley and Mr.
Petrie,

Petrie, that the Company have acquired an acceſſion of territory, the net revenue of which amounted to thirty-nine lacks and fifty thouſand rupees.

N° III.

" *Madras*, 21ſt *Feb.* 1792.

" It ought to be obſerved, that the re-
" ſiſtance, on the part of the enemy, was
" conducted with more ſkill and intrepi-
" dity, than has ever marked the conduct
" of the armies of Hindoſtan on any for-
" mer occaſion. The ultimate exertions
" of the Sultaun were ſuch, as deſpair ge-
" nerally dictates to proud and unrelent-
" ing ſpirits."

Another writer from Madras, during the firſt campaign touches on the opinion then

entertained

tertained of Tippoo's abilities, and on the probability of his future deftiny.

" *Madras*, 16th *May* 1791.

" To what region the Sultaun can poffi-
" bly fly, after the fall of his capital,
" and his Beddanore poffeffions, is matter
" of much conjecture among the QUID-
" NUNCS of the Eaft. He can find no
" afylum with the Polygars. While he
" retains a part of his treafure, a force will
" be at his command, fufficient to fecure a
" temporary retreat among the hills. Some
" fage politicians fend him to *Mecca*,
" others to *Pondicherry*.

" What human ability can effect, Tippoo
" will perform. He has certainly fhewn
" himfelf a man of fuperior talents, and a
" determined foldier."

N° IV.

" *Madras,* 24*th Feb.* 1792.

" It remains a queſtion for politicians to
" diſcuſs, Whether we ought to have ſtopt
" ſhort of the entire ſubverſion of Tippoo's
" empire, when we undoubtedly poſſeſſed
" the means of accompliſhing it; or whe-
" ther it is a better policy to let it exiſt,
" reducing it in ſuch a degree, as to ren-
" der it no longer formidable to the Eng-
" liſh intereſts, while it may ſerve as a
" counterpoiſe to the other great Powers
" in India? Time, and the events of the
" eighteenth century, can only ſolve this
" intricate problem.

" Since the buſineſs has now terminated,
" I have but one wiſh, which is, that our
" noble

" noble Peer may acquire as much credit
" from his country, for the peace he has
" made, as he has derived glory from the
" conduct of the war."

The liberal wiſh of this Gentleman muſt, without doubt, be ſoon and moſt completely gratified : for, while no former war with the MYSOREAN SOVEREIGN, either redounded much to our credit, or terminated without a heavy load of financial incumbrance, the preſent war ſeems to be deciſive, has been conducted with unprecedented œconomy, and has terminated in the ſecurity of our frontiers, and in a large increaſe of revenue and dominion.

The affairs of the India Company, now rendered in all reſpects ſo flouriſhing, may acquire addicional proſperity from a commercial treaty with the Chineſe Empire.

G

pire. The embaſſy of Lord Macartney, which is directed to that object, will infallibly be conducted with ability and profound diſcernment: And whatever may be the reſult of this deſign with regard to the commerce of the Eaſt, it is likely to be productive of uſeful diſcovery, and of eminent advantage to the learned world.

THE END.

www.ingramcontent.com/pod-product-compliance
Lightning Source LLC
Chambersburg PA
CBHW021438090426
42739CB00009B/1542